Zoom in

Contents

Food	4
Shells	6
Wings	8
Fish	10
Gardens	12
Rain	14
Cameras	18
Patterns	22

Written by Liz Miles

Collins

Record fantastic patterns with a camera.

looking down at a mushroom

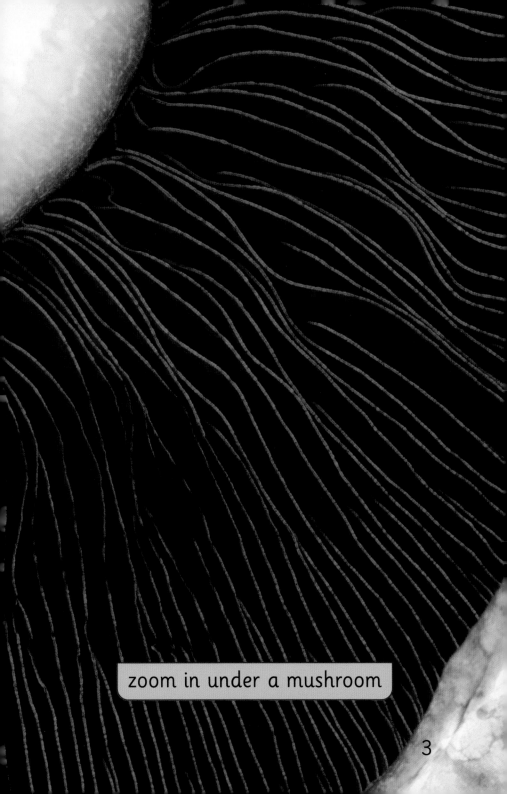

zoom in under a mushroom

3

Food

Look for lighter and darker patterns in food.

Look at the rings in a carrot.

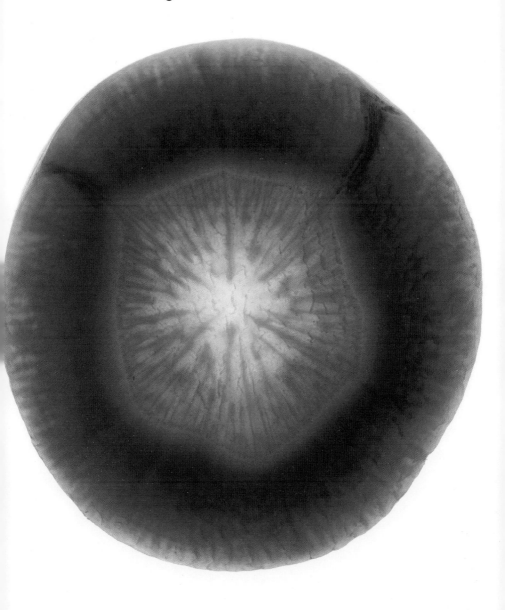

Shells

Look for shells with coiling patterns.

Pick up shells with fan patterns.

Wings

Quick! Get a shot of a pair of wings!

kingfisher

fan pattern

This moth wing has patterns, too.

Fish

Look for patterns on fish.

Zoom in nearer. This fish shimmers in the light.

Gardens

See patterns in ferns, roots and weeds.

Get near for shots of seeds.

Rain

A camera can record patterns in the rain.

Getting nearer, we can zoom in and see this ...

You can zoom in too!

Cameras

A big lens gets nearer shots of things.

lens

This is a good camera, too.

Get near to pick up patterns.

Zoom in with the fingers to see them better.

Patterns

Review: After reading

Use your assessment from hearing the children read to choose any GPCs, words or tricky words that need additional practice.

Read 1: Decoding

- On page 8, point to the word **shot**. Ask the children what this word means, and to check their answer by seeing if it makes sense in the sentence. Discuss how **Get a shot** means take a picture/photo.
- Ask the children to sound out these words. Ask: Which has the short /**oo**/ sound? (*looking, look*)
  looking   food   too   zoom   look   roots
- Ask the children to read page 16. Challenge them to sound out the words silently to encourage fluency. Say: Can you blend the words in your head when you read this page?

Read 2: Prosody

- Turn to pages 8 and 9. Discuss the punctuation.
  o Point to the exclamation mark. Ask: What feeling should we put in our voice for this exclamation? (e.g. *excitement, urgency*)
  o Point to the comma and remind the children that we pause at a comma.
- Ask the children to read the pages, using expression and pauses.
- Bonus content: Ask the children to read pages 18 to 21 as if they were presenting a children's programme about photography. Encourage them to use emphasis to make the instructions clear.

Read 3: Comprehension

- Look at the front and back cover pictures. Ask: What would you like to take photos of?
- Ask the children: What do all the photos show? (*patterns*) What is the book about? (*how cameras can record "fantastic patterns"*) If necessary reread page 2 and discuss how this introduces the theme.
- Turn to page 5 and point to the word **rings**. Ask: What other similar words could we use instead here?
- Turn to pages 22–23 and invite the children to talk about what patterns they can see and what they think they are.
- Bonus content: Ask the children to look at pages 18 to 21 and discuss how they might use the different cameras. What might they like to take pictures of, and which camera would they like to use?